Reflections

of a

Searching Heart

Reflections

of a

Searching Heart

J. F. Brindley

iUniverse, Inc.
Bloomington

Reflections of a Searching Heart

iUniverse books may be ordered through booksellers or by contacting:

iUniverse
1663 Liberty Drive
Bloomington, IN 47403
www.iuniverse.com
1-800-Authors (1-800-288-4677)

ISBN: 978-1-4502-8094-5 (sc)
ISBN: 978-1-4502-8096-9 (ebook)
ISBN: 978-1-4502-8095-2 (dj)

Library of Congress Control Number: 2010918875

Printed in the United States of America

iUniverse rev. date: 2/17/2011

For Frances, Bret, Reese, Rebecca, Cooper,
and Alexis, my six grandchildren.

For the Searchers Sunday School Class
and Christ Church United Methodist,
Birmingham, Alabama.

Acknowledgments

I offer my thanks for the writers of the Old and New Testament, for their willingness to record our past so they could affect our development and so that we can, in turn, shape our future.

Table of Contents

Introduction

A Searcher

I am a searcher, searching for God's truth.
I've been a searcher since my youth.

I've searched my world and I've searched my heart.
I've been searching to find what part
I am to play in my earthly time,
but I know I've been given the gift of rhyme.

Finally I came to believe that my verse
was God's gift for me to share and converse.
I began writing about what I could feel
when I studied the Bible and let God reveal
His truth to me, in ways I could express—
in rhymed couplet, no less.

If these poems give your spirits a lift,
know 'twas God who gave me this special gift!
Praise Him and worship our God up above
for these poems that I submit with His love.

BIBLE STORIES

Genesis 1:1–31
2:1–25

Creation

A God too amazing for us to understand
created the sky, the sea, and the land.
He created all plant life, fruit, and flowers.
This creation was done in just a few hours.
Next, He filled the sea, the land, and the sky
with animals that could swim, run, and fly.
God knew it was time, so he created man
to have dominion over sky, sea, and land.
Carefully he picked up a hand full of sod,
and man was molded by our glorious God.
It was God's own breath that man first breathed,
and the name "Adam" from God he received.

Now, Adam was given an important task—
to name all the animals from the first to the last.
All the animals in the air, on the land, and below
were lined up by God in one very long row.
Every size, shape, and color was represented by God's creatures—
whether tiny, gigantic, bright colored, or muted their features.
Each animal presented himself in all of his splendor,
patiently waiting for Adam his name to render.

The mighty lion with his magnificent mane
was standing in line behind the whooping crane.
The kangaroo, the beaver, and the koala bear
were careful not to step on the turtle or the hare.
From muskrat, bobcat, tsetse fly, and toad,
to elephant and inch worm their names from Adam flowed.
Their names were as different as every animal's shape—
the penguin, toucan, the horse, and the ape.
The many colorful creatures delighted Adam's eyes.
God had chosen colors to sparkle or disguise.

Adam loved the blue of the peacock and the gray of the slug,
the yellow canary, and the black dotted ladybug,
the red of the fox, the bright green of the parrot,
the pink of the flamingo, the soft brown of the ferret,
the sleek black panther, the snow-white swan,
the striped zebra, and the chameleon.
The line seemed to be moving very, very slowly,
through dragonfly, magpie, centipede, and crow.
Finally, Adam came to the end of the line.
The very last animal he named "porcupine."

The newly named animals spread throughout the earth,
and many were soon waiting their first baby's birth.
Only Adam was left completely alone,
so while Adam slept, God took one rib bone
from Adam's side, and created a new life.
God named her Eve and made her Adam's wife.
Dear God, we give you all of our praise
for the world you created in just six short days.

Notes

Exodus 2:1–10

Out from the Water

The little reed basket floated in the Nile.
Inside slept a blessed and beautiful child.
A desperate mother stood on the shore
and prayed as she had never prayed before.
This plan had come to her in a dream—
put the babe in a basket and float him downstream.
Now she reflected on what she had done.
Had she thrown away her own infant son?
The tar and pitch on the boat might leak;
the baby could drown while it was asleep.
What if the basket turned over or sank?
All these thoughts came as she stood on the bank.
She knew that the river was a dangerous place
and she had acted in such great haste.
What if Pharaoh's daughter didn't come today?
Or if the basket was ignored or just pushed away?
Her daughter Miriam watched the small boat,
as it bobbled and rocked but somehow stayed afloat.
She hurried away to pray and weep all alone.
It was the saddest moment she'd ever known.

Miriam waited and watched, for hours, it seemed.
As the day grew warmer, inside the basket it steamed.
A crocodile eyed the basket as it slowly slid by.
Now Miriam prayed the babe wouldn't wake and cry.
The sun's boiling heat was directly overhead,
when Pharaoh's daughter came, dressed in purple and red.
Her giggling servant girls were leading the way
down to the water's edge to bathe on that day.
"Bring me that basket, the one half hidden by the reeds,"
Pharaoh's daughter commanded as the girls tended her needs.
One sturdy servant lifted the basket from the water
and carefully carried it to the feet of Pharaoh's daughter.
Removing the lid, the servant drew back and sighed.

All were amazed to see the baby inside.
Miriam held her breath and she closed her eyes.
Pharaoh's daughter would determine if the baby lived or died.
Miriam thought of her most daring mother
who'd trusted this Egyptian princess would love Miriam's brother.
The plan had seemed so wonderful just yesterday.
but now Miriam feared she should just run away.

Carefully lifting the baby from its little cradle boat,
Pharaoh's daughter suddenly felt a catch in her throat.
It was a Hebrew baby boy—she could see by its dress—
but he was beautiful as he opened his mouth to express
his unhappiness at someone for disturbing his rest,
for his frets became loud cries and tears ran from his eyes.
"Hot, hungry, wet, and scared, I do surmise."
Pharaoh's daughter, to soothe the baby, tried
to hold him close and pat his sweet head.
"He is a gift from the gods," she said.
"But he is a Hebrew," one servant boldly declared.
"Hebrew baby boys are not to be spared."
She had heard her father's edict to kill Hebrew boys,
but until now her father's edict had only been noise.
She knew the number of slaves worried him.
By murdering their male babies, he could control them.
"This gift given to me will not be denied.
This babe is now my son and with me will abide."
She clutched the baby tighter and said nothing more.
She could manage her father; she had done it before.

Now Miriam left her hiding place,
and, nearing Pharaoh's daughter, she fell on her face.
"Great One, send me to find a wet nurse for him."
The Egyptians were deadly quiet—not a sound came from them.
Finally, Pharaoh's daughter said, "Rise and speak to me.
Why, you are only a child yourself, I see."
"Great One, many a Hebrew mother has lost her son.
If you will send me, I will find a special one

to nurse the baby as if he were her own
and then return him when he is near grown."
"Oh, yes, I'm quite sure what you say is true;
go now and hurry; I'll wait here for you."
Miriam ran as quickly as a deer.
She left so fast that she didn't hear
a servant request to follow the child
to find the Hebrew mother so full of guile
that she would tempt Pharaoh's daughter this way,
but Pharaoh's daughter knew just what to say.
"The woman who comes will protect the child
and return him to me in a very short while."

Now Miriam and her mother neared.
Pharaoh's daughter at the Hebrew woman peered.
"The gods have given this child to me.
He needs a wet nurse, as you can see.
Can you perform this important task?"
'Twas the question Pharaoh's daughter asked.
"Oh, yes, Great One, it would be my joy
to nurse and care for this baby boy."
"Then take him home and I'll provide
for him as long as he does abide
in your care, but prepare my son for the day
when he returns to me to stay."
She took a ring from her right hand
and strung it on a leather band.
"Put this ring on the babe's neck to signify
to Pharaoh's soldiers he is not to die."
His true mother took the babe into her open arms.
Gone now were all her mother's fears and alarms.
She knew her son would live to become a man,
but his importance she didn't yet understand.

What she did know was that her God was good.
She remembered the spot on the bank where she'd stood
and prayed that her child would be spared,

but she most certainly was not prepared
to see her child, who'd been condemned to die,
raised up and accepted by Egypt's most high,
not as a servant but as an adopted son
whose life of great privilege had just begun.
Her day, begun in the dawn with fear and tribulation,
had ended at dusk with joy and elation.
God had answered her prayers and more,
for her faithfulness and trust had meant a downpour
of blessings from the Holy Father above
to prove to her, and to us, the power of God's love.

Notes

Daniel 6:1–22

The Lion's Den

In the Old Testament, Daniel was put in the lion's den,
his love and prayers to his God—his only sin.
Daniel knew he would live if it were God's will.
If he died, he knew he was God's child still.
He sank to his knees and began to pray,
thanking God for His blessings that very day.
Now, God closed the mouths of those hungry beasts.
That was totally out of the lion's character, to say the least.
Those powerful jaws and huge dangerous paws
were made to clutch and devour any and all who dared
to approach and enter their blood-drenched lair.
But, now gentle, these lions curled around Daniel's feet,
and Daniel lay amidst them to go to sleep.
While Daniel and the lions peacefully slept,
his family and friends quietly prayed and wept.
They prayed that God would somehow let Daniel survive,
but they were amazed when Daniel walked out alive.
"How did you do it?" they asked of him.
"I did nothing; it was God who answered our prayers," he told them.

Have you ever been in a lion's den?
You may answer no, but I ask you about when …
you got caught between two warring friends,
each expecting to be the one you defend.
Or when your adult children expect your total support
of their decisions, when you believe they're at fault?
Have you ever felt your job was eating you alive
by an eighty-hour week instead of the promised nine to five?
Have you ever caused dissension by a stand you took?
Expecting approval—not expecting that dirty look!
Have you ever been cornered and forced to choose
blindly, without knowing if you will win or lose?
Have you ever been pushed by conflicting beliefs
when your mind and your soul each seeks

the answers and choices you will have to make
when the central core of your being is at stake?
If you have ever faced these challenges, my friend,
you have certainly been in the lion's den.

I don't expect Daniel really knew why God placed him,
a true believer and servant, in a place so grim.
But I believe Daniel's life is a lesson God's taught again and again—
that He's in control right now, just as back then.
We just need to get out of his way and put our faith in Him.
At times He will send pelting rain, heavy snow, and mighty wind,
but they are just reminders that we depend on him.
When we pray, He will deliver us from the horrible places we are in
and will ultimately take us home to be with Him.

Notes

Genesis 37:1–16
39:1–23
40:1–23
41:1–57

The Coat

It was a coat fit for a king.
Young Joseph had not ever seen
any garment made to equal it.
For him, it was a perfect fit.
It draped from his shoulders down
until it almost touched the ground,
and its true colors were as bright
as the dazzling noonday sunlight.
Blood red stripes and rich cobalt blue,
amber and purple and emerald green, too.
Joseph's coat was beyond compare,
and left his older brothers to stare
as Joseph walked around and about
displaying his favored position, no doubt,
for this gift from his father made it clear
that Joseph was the son Jacob held most dear.

Now jealousy began to fill his brothers' hearts,
but true hatred for Joseph really starts
when Joseph tells them of his dreams.
His brothers will bow down to him it seems!
These older boys are incensed and mystified
by the depth of their younger brother's pride.
What leads him to believe he would become
anything more than the eleventh son
of a gentle shepherd—older now and content,
but a shepherd who lives in a desert tent.
They laugh at Joseph's silly pipe dream,
but events are coming that can't be foreseen.

It begins on a quiet, ordinary day.
The older brothers have traveled away
caring for the flocks in a distant place,
when Joseph sees concern on Jacob's face.

It was an ordinary request.
"I am concerned, I must confess,"
Jacob says to Joseph. "It's been too long—
I fear that something must be wrong.
Search for your brothers and return to me
with news of what the trouble may be."
The boy of seventeen is filled with pride
that his aging father on him relies.
He puts on his coat of many colors
so he'll stand out from all the others.
He travels the way the flocks have gone
hoping to find his brothers before long.

His brothers see Joseph from far away.
"Look whose coming to visit us today.
It's the dreamer in his stinking coat.
I imagine he's coming this way to gloat,"
says one brother with hate in his eyes.
Quickly they all began to realize
they could kill Joseph far from their father's eyes.
Only Reuben tries to find a compromise:
"Just throw him into that cistern until he dies.
Don't put our brother's blood on our hands."
They all agree this is the best of plans.
They fall on Joseph as soon as he arrives;
they tear his coat from his body and he tries
to fight back, but they are too many, too strong,
and it doesn't take them very long
until they drop Joseph into the dry well.
It's a deep, damp, and dirty cell.
If they plan to kill him, Joseph cannot tell.

He's hurt; he's in shock and tries to cry out,
"Keep my coat, if that's what this is about.
Just pull me up and I'll tell Father it's lost.
I'll never tell into this well I was tossed."
But his brothers don't answer him at all,

and move away from the cistern wall.
They sit to have their evening meal,
each one unsure of what he should feel,
when suddenly another, better answer appears—
a caravan on the way to Egypt nears.
Now, Judah says, "Let's sell Joseph to these men.
Then we'll never have to see him again."
He doesn't have to die, they suddenly realize,
and the sin of Cain won't stain their lives.
So Joseph is pulled up from the well
and taken to the caravan to sell.

They receive eight ounces of silver for their brother
and see Joseph look from one of them to the other.
His eyes look sad, but he doesn't talk
as he is tied to a camel and told to walk.
He doesn't look back as he leaves them behind.
Perhaps, they thought, killing him would have been more kind.
But, after dipping the coat in a goat's blood
and dragging it through dirt and mud,
they hurry to their father's side.
"We found this coat on the road," they lie.
"Is this young Joseph's coat?" they inquire.
Now Jacob's eyes are old and tired,
but he knows this coat; it is the one
he had given to Joseph, his favored son.
He cries out in overwhelming grief—
for it is now his true belief
that Joseph has been killed by a hungry beast.
Over time his mourning never ceased,
but his brothers think Joseph is forever gone
from their lives—but they were so wrong.

It's hard to imagine a worse place for Joseph to be—
a teenage slave in Egypt, an idol-worshipping country.
But God was never far from the side
of young Joseph, who on his God relied.

First, sold to a captain in Pharaoh's army,
he studied and learned and grew to be
the overseer of his owner's entire property.
He was as trusted as a slave could be.
Grown now and handsome, he attracted the captain's wife,
but he avoided her; he knew she could destroy his life.
Angry, she accused Joseph of attacking her,
and her husband believed it did occur.

Joseph was thrown into prison, although innocent,
but he didn't curse God for where he'd been sent
or the unfair treatment he had again received.
He could have given up and just grieved,
but instead he befriended the prison guard
and over all of the prisoners he was put in charge.
Years passed and he lingered in that gruesome place,
his youth disappearing; his life a waste.
But he never believed God had abandoned him
to live and die in a dungeon so dim.
One day there was an unusual event—
two of Pharaoh's household to the prison were sent.
His cupbearer and baker had offended him
and Pharaoh, in his reckless anger, imprisoned them
in this filthy, flea-ridden, foul-smelling den
of helpless low-lifes, slaves, and dishonest men.
The prison guards assigned Joseph to tend their needs,
and in this impossible task he somehow succeeded.
He befriended the two and earned their trust,
and one day he heard them openly discuss
the strange dreams that each has dreamed.
They needed a dream interpreter, it seemed.

"God will allow me to interpret for you,"
Joseph told those high-ranking two.

On hearing their dreams, Joseph was careful to relate
to the cupbearer that in only three days Pharaoh would reinstate
him to his place of prominence and respect,
but, alas, the baker in three days would hang from the neck.
Joseph's interpretation indeed occurred on the third day.
It was exactly as he stated and exactly that way.
Joseph had asked the cupbearer to remember Joseph's plight
when the cupbearer regained Pharaoh's favor and sight.
But two more long years came and went,
and the cupbearer never even thought of or sent
for Joseph, the young innocent Hebrew slave
until the day, the cupbearer heard the Pharaoh rave
that no one had been able to explain the meaning
of the strange and troublesome dreams he'd been dreaming.
Pharaoh knew it was important for him to find out
exactly what these dreams had been all about.
Suddenly the cupbearer had a clear vision
of the prisoner Joseph and he made a decision.
He told Pharaoh he had known an imprisoned Hebrew
whose dream interpretations had always come true.

In desperation Pharaoh sent for this man
and finally before Pharaoh Joseph came to stand.
Pharaoh said, "You are a prisoner in a foreign land
but my cupbearer believes that you can
interpret my dreams; tell me what the meaning can be."
"It is not I, but God will tell me,"
Joseph answered as he began to pray
that God would hear him and tell him what to say.
On hearing Pharaoh's dreams, for Joseph the meaning was clear
and he gave Pharaoh the answer he needed to hear.
"For seven years Egypt's harvest will be bountiful.
Your kingdom will prosper, but you must be careful,
for seven years of total famine is bound to follow.

For nothing that is planted those years will grow.
Since Pharaoh's dream was doubled there is no doubt.
God's will is set; it will come about.
Starvation will occur throughout the land
unless Pharaoh can select a capable man
to store one fifth of each good year's grain
in storehouses where it must remain
until the ground's fertile soil disappears
and begins those dreaded lean years.
Then grain can be provided by Pharaoh's decree
to all of Egypt's people who are hungry."
After hearing Joseph's words, Pharaoh was relieved.
Joseph's dream interpretation Pharaoh completely believed.
The plan that Joseph proposed Pharaoh conceived
as the answer God had given. It could be achieved
if Joseph were chosen and put in command
only second to Pharaoh in all the land.
And so by decree, Pharaoh elevated Joseph's station
and made him second ruler over the whole nation.
Pharaoh gave him a signet ring from Pharaoh's own hand,
and gold-threaded linen clothes that were even more grand
than the coat of many colors, the coat of Joseph's youth.
It was only now that Joseph began to see the truth.
God had chosen this unusually difficult way
to bring Joseph to this momentous day.
He'd been in Egypt for thirteen years,
and had learned to overcome any fears
by relying on his God to provide
for him and always be his guide.
He knew not what lay ahead,
but he knew his God had led
him and would remain at his side
as long as his heart didn't fill with pride.

This story has many chapters more.
I've only partially opened the door,
But in this part that I have retold
You have seen how God's plans unfold.
They are often not as we expect them to be,
but remember, we can only partially see.
If God is given free reign in our lives,
and to love and obey him each of us tries,
God's rewards will rain down from above
and encase us all in his unfailing love.

Acts: 2–4
6–8:1–4
9:1–31

Witness

After Pentecost the number of Jesus' followers grew.
The High Priest and the Sanhedrin didn't know what to do.
First Peter and John were arrested, but to no avail.
One Pharisee said, "If they are truly men of God, they will not fail."

This convinced the Sanhedrin to wait and see
if it were truly God's son who had died on Calvary's tree.
So both apostles were flogged, chastised but not killed.
When released, their teaching and preaching were not stilled.

Then one man, Stephen, filled with God's grace and power
began making converts hour after hour.
Suddenly Stephen was seen as the Sanhedrin's main enemy.
He was arrested and charged with preaching blasphemy.

Now, Saul, a devoted and learned Pharisee
who hated this Jesus from Galilee,
heard of the charges to be made at Stephen's trial.
His mouth filled with bitter tasting bile.

He determined to be there and hear Stephen confess
his lies and his fake miracles, no less.
So Saul was there and heard Stephen proclaim
words that would this court inflame.
Stephen cried, "Jesus was sent by God to this earth;
Jesus was the Messiah from the day of his humble birth."

Saul's hatred for Stephen and all Jesus' followers burned.
It was for revenge Saul's heart churned.
He called out with all the Sanhedrin and joined the throng
of those who were determined to right this wrong.

They dragged Stephen out and threw him down
outside the city on the rough, rocky ground.
They were going to stone Stephen without delay.
He was unfit to live another day.

As they searched for sharp rocks in the oppressive heat,
they took off their coats and put them at the feet
of Saul, who gave his approval of this punishment
for the Jesus follower who wouldn't repent.

The stones began pelting Stephen's body and face.
When he began praying, they picked up the pace.
Stephen cried out, "Lord, Jesus receive my spirit."
The rock throwers didn't want to hear it.

So his mouth became the focus of the stones.
He continued to pray aloud without any groans.
"Lord, do not hold this sin against them,"
were the last words that came from him.

He closed his eyes and fell asleep.
But, his apparent death didn't keep
the rocks from continuing to rain down,
until Stephen's blood covered the ground.
The hot red blood spattered all about
until of Stephen's death there was no doubt.

Panic swept through the converted Jews.
Their lives they didn't want to lose.
They left Jerusalem and scattered far and wide,
but Saul wouldn't let them quietly hide.

He began searching throughout the land
and bringing to prison every converted woman and man
he could find to prevent them from teaching that God's son
had died for the sins of everyone.

But Saul didn't forget how Stephen had died.
It was so clear that Stephen relied
on this Jesus to take him to Heaven above
where he'd live forever, surrounded by eternal love.

This kind of faith was hard for Saul to conceive.
He wondered how Jesus' followers could believe
that God's son was a poor man, a humble carpenter—
not a priest, but a man who would surrender
his life and die as a Roman prisoner, crucified
with a common criminal on either side.

Saul was determined he would not rest
until all Jesus' followers were made to confess
their sin and return to the Law of Moses
and the rules for living that the law imposes.

'Twas on the road to Damascus, when Saul
saw a bright light, heard Jesus' voice, and did fall
to the ground, blinded and totally surprised,
that this Pharisee Saul came to realize
that Jesus was truly God's beloved Son—
the risen Savior, the Prince of Peace, the promised one.

Jesus words, "Saul, Saul, why do you persecute me?"
meant that, although blind, Saul could finally see
why Stephen and the others were so willing to die
for Jesus who now spoke to Saul from Heaven, above the sky.

Saul became Paul, a sinner transformed by grace
into God's greatest witness over time and space.
The writer of letters all Christians cherish—
a missionary, a teacher, a preacher who would perish.

For the witnessing he continued to do,
and the example his life has meant for me and you.
Most of us have not been asked to die for our belief.
No rock throwers have knocked out our teeth.

Few if any have been struck blind
by a bolt of bright light or any kind
of booming voice from heaven that questions us
about our choices and our lack of trust.

A Stephen or a Paul we may never be,
but we as Christians can agree
that we learn from our ignorance, our failures, and mistakes.
And know that our blessed Jesus always takes
our hand, and directs our path to show us the way
to serve him and to witness for him each and every day.

Christmas Stories

Luke 2:1–20
Matthew 2:1–23

The Light

Lights began twinkling far down the road.
The little donkey swayed beneath its load.
The young girl pulled her thin cloak up tight.
There was a chill in the air that night.

The road had been busy throughout the day.
Many were traveling the very same way.
A girl on a donkey with a man walking alongside
couldn't keep pace with the clamoring tide.

Pushed aside by ox-carts and caravans of spitting camels,
they barely missed getting caught in the briars and brambles.
They had stopped to drink from a cool flowing stream.
They had stopped to hear a yellow bird sing.

They had finally stopped to rest 'neath an olive tree—
a much needed rest for a mother-to-be.
When they finally passed through the town's old gate,
they found they had arrived far too late.

At each inn they were turned away.
There was no place where they could stay.
Joseph closed his eyes and said a short prayer
when Mary said, "Look, there's an inn over there."

The innkeeper had just shut his door tight,
but, hearing a tap, he came out with a light.
He saw the woman's tired but beautiful face.
"Follow me," he said, "I know of a place."

He led them down a dark winding street.
"Here in this stable you are welcome to sleep."
It was dreary and dank and just a cowshed,
but it had a roof and sweet-smelling straw for a bed.
Mary sank down on the bed Joseph made.
"Thank you, dear Lord," both of them prayed.
The donkey ate some of the hay he had found.
A cow stood by, but made not a sound.

There was dancing and music throughout the town,
and nobody heard the baby's first sound
but Mary and Joseph, who rejoiced at his birth,
and the angels in Heaven sang of peace on Earth.

Mary counted his fingers and counted his toes.
She marveled at his eyes and his mouth like a rose.
She saw him smile, then close his eyes to sleep.
She kissed his closed eyes and then his soft cheek.

Both parents were watching him peacefully sleep
when they heard a very loud bleat.
Sheep were coming into the cowshed,
and all settled down 'round the babe's manger bed.

Shepherds with sheep dogs pushed into the shed too,
and one spoke out loud, "Oh, look it's true."
Mary and Joseph were in shock and surprise.
"Why are you here?" Mary finally cried.

"Angels appeared in the sky up above,
and told us of God's unfailing love.
We trembled and shook with obvious fear,
then the angels were gone and a star did appear."

"We followed the star like the angels had said,
and to the birthplace of our Savior it carefully led."
Mary and Joseph looked straight overhead
and, yes, a large bright star shone over the shed.

The shepherds stayed until the sun lit the day,
then slowly and silently they crept away.
The townspeople saw the star shining so bright,
it made the sun pale in its glorious light.

But the townspeople were busy, don't you know.
They had work to do and places to go.
Stars in the sky were where stars had always been.
Stranger things had happened—now and again.

But the star remained both day and night,
and soon it became a quite normal sight.
Even these shepherds started to forget
the angels' song and what the angels' song meant.

But God had another plan for this star,
for wise men saw it in a land afar.
They knew it marked a special event.
They knew a king from heaven was sent.

They studied the star and made calculations.
They conferred with each other then made preparations.
They journeyed across the hot desert sand
to visit the newborn King in his homeland.

The star stayed before them and led the way
'til finally in Judea they stopped one day.
"Oh, where can we find the newborn King?"
They asked everyone they met the very same thing.

Now, King Herod ruled Judea during those years,
and losing his throne was one of his fears.
When he heard of the words being asked by the three,
he said, "Send the high priests to me."

"Where will the Christ Child be born?" he asked them.
"The prophets have written it will be Bethlehem,"
the priests answered quickly and then disappeared.
It was King Herod's temper that they most feared.

But Herod was crafty and he kept his head.
He sent for the wise men and to them he said,
"This new baby King has been hidden away,
but he hides in Bethlehem I've been told today.

"I'm sure you will find him in such a small town.
Even I want to worship him when he is found.
Return to me when you find that dear one.
I'll treat him just like he was my true son."

The wise men left for Bethlehem that same night.
They wanted to arrive before daylight.
They came to the town still following the star.
It led them to a place with a door left ajar.

They entered and saw a babe all aglow.
The starlight encircled his head like a halo.
The wise men knew this was the King they sought.
This was the miracle about which they had taught.

The parents looked pleased that the wise men were here.
They welcomed them in and let them draw near.
Baby Jesus was smiling and reached out his hands.
It certainly looked like he understands.

The wise men unwrapped three pouches of fur
and presented three gifts—gold, frankincense, and myrrh.
The parents were overcome with total surprise.
They had never seen such gifts in their lives.

They thanked the wise men and then Mary wept.
It was left to Joseph the gifts to accept.
The wise men explained it was they who'd been blessed.
They had proved that the star was the sign they'd professed.

'Twas now that the wise men again proved they were wise,
for they knew that King Herod had spoken lies.
When they left, they traveled far from Herod's court.
They didn't return; they didn't report.

But even these wise men didn't know
to what level of evil Herod would go.
But God knew of Herod's very black heart
and in this story, God plays the main part.

God spoke to Joseph in a dream that night,
and told him it was time to take flight.
"Herod's soldiers are coming with swords and knives
and when they find male babies they will take their lives.

"Go to Egypt with Mary and take the child.
You will need to stay for quite awhile."
So Joseph woke Mary and they prepared to flee.
They packed their few belongings on the little donkey.

"How far away is Egypt?" Mary wanted to know.
"It doesn't matter," Joseph answered, "God says we must go.
We'll escape tonight for it's as dark as can be.
Look, Mary, the star is no longer shining, you see?"

The light was living in the baby now.
And when he grew up, Jesus would teach us how
each of us can shine ever so bright;
can be a star, can be a light.

The Christmas story is over two thousand years old,
but I love to hear it each time it is told.
How Jesus came as a babe from Heaven above,
to light the world with God's eternal love.

Notes

The following poem includes events not found in the Bible. However, on such a miraculous night, the writer believes they could have occurred.

The Night

The old cow munched on the hay.
It was stale, but she liked it that way.
A small mouse scurried across the floor.
He liked the night because he got to explore.
A sleepy barn cat opened a big sleepy eye
and decided to just let the mouse slip by.
That mouse would always return to its nest,
and for now the cat could continue to rest.

Through a hole in the old leaky roof above
suddenly swooped in a perfectly white dove.
It found a spot on a rafter to perch.
It looked all around; its eyes seemed to search,
but it finally settled in and began to softly coo.
The old cow liked the sound and began to quietly moo.
The cat wondered why they were disturbing her peaceful rest,
but the sounds were pleasing, she had to confess.

Then an unexpected noise and a very bright light
changed forever what had started as a typical night.
A man, a woman, and a little donkey came into this place.
It was a dark, dank, and unwelcoming space.
This stable had been neglected for a very long time,
but for God's purpose this place was sublime.
The young girl spoke in a voice ever so kind,
"It's a dry place and it's all we can find."

The man looked concerned and he looked all around.
He said, "It's the only place left in the town."
"Joseph, we'll be very comfortable here," she replied.
She sank down on an old milking stool she'd spied.
He unpacked the donkey and offered Mary some honey and bread.
She shook her head and asked for water instead.
He led the little donkey into an empty stall;
that exhausted donkey looked ready to fall.

The dove and the cow were very quiet now,
but noise and the light had awakened the sow.
Her six little piglets began squealing in a most discordant way.
The donkey didn't like that sound and he began to bray.
The other animals became restless and began moving around,
but the young girl wasn't bothered at all by the sound.
She picked up one piglet and hugged it tight;
it soon fell asleep and slept all the night.

When she placed it back by its mother to sleep,
the five other piglets made not another peep.
And now the barn cat walked right up to her.
She picked it up, stroked it, and it began to purr.
The donkey's braying stopped when from high above
he saw the perfectly white dove.
And so order was easily and quickly restored
for God's love and peace over this stable was poured.

A few hours passed and the animals perked up their ears.
They found it hard to believe the sounds each one hears.
A baby had been born and was making baby noise,
those special newborn sounds that everyone enjoys.
Its mother, Mary, was busy with her new mother chores.
Her humble surroundings she just simply ignored.
She wrapped the baby in the special clothes she has brought,
and her husband, Joseph, suddenly had an excellent thought.

The old abandoned manger pushed up against the donkey stall,
he filled it with fresh hay and on top of it he placed Mary's shawl.
The manger had become a perfect baby bed
where the newborn baby Jesus could rest his sweet head.
Now the perfectly white dove began his descent,
for it was for Jesus' birth he had been sent.
He slowly circled and circled this holy newborn,
then perched on the manger he'd been sent to adorn.

Yes, this perfectly white dove had been sent from above
to show the world God's gift of perfect love.
Soon several shepherds quietly came through the door
followed by their sheep, a dozen or more.
The small stable seemed to grow to the size it needed to be
to accommodate all who wanted to see
this very precious little holy stranger
who was quietly sleeping now in the old manger.

The shepherds mumbled about the birth of the Prince of Peace.
It was these words that gave the perfectly white dove his release.
So up and out the old leaky hole in the roof he flew.
The old cow gave him a good-bye moo.
'Twas followed by an oink, a bray, a squeak, and a mew.
A baa from the sheep caused the sheep dog to bark,
and believe it or not, that was the spark!
Now all of the animals began to make loud noise,
but somehow their sound was now the sounds of joys.

For the mouse squeak became the sound of the piccolo;
the donkey's bray sounded like the banjo.
The sow's musical voice sounded like the trombone,
and the cat joined in like a saxophone.
The five little piglets' voices became five clarinets.
The sixth one was still sleeping from Mary's gentle pats.
The sheep dog's shrill bark had become jingling bells.
He felt great pride, but his head never swelled.
The sheep's baas were united to become a bass drum.
It was their job to keep the group's rhythm.

Now all of these instruments hadn't been invented yet on Earth,
but God sent this very special music for His Son's birth.
The music excelled all music created by mortal men,
those alive now and those way back then.
Even the animals knew their sounds were splendid,
and they continued their concert until the night ended.
When the sun appeared and lit the day,

the shepherds and their flocks crept silently away.
The animals, all tired, closed their eyes to sleep.
'Twas a much needed sleep that was so very deep
they only awoke when the day came to an end.
Each one was looking forward for their music to begin.

But, when the donkey opened his mouth to play—
Oops! There only came out a bray.
The old cow's moo had returned in full force,
and the piglets' high-pitched squeals were not a chorus.
The same old meow came from the lazy cat,
and the tiny little squeak was, of course, the rat.
The old sow knew her beautiful voice was gone,
and all of the animals wondered what had gone wrong.

Well, that wonderful night had come and gone,
and now it appeared the world would just continue on.
For the animals sounded like animals again,
and the shepherds and their flocks were in the hills where they'd been.
The animals quickly forgot the music they'd made,
and the shepherd's memories of the angels began to fade.

But the world was different, as we all know,
for the baby Jesus grew up and made it so.
He taught us to love and care for each other,
and to treat every man as our brother.
He died for our sins; he took them away,
and told us we'd join Him in Heaven someday.
Thank you, dear Lord, for sending the world your Son.
We honor Him each year with this Christmas celebration.

Easter Stories

Luke 19:29–38
Matthew 21:1–11

It was Just a Donkey

It was just a donkey,
not a fiery stallion with flashing eyes
whose speed and agility any prince would prize.

It was just a donkey,
not a majestic camel traveling without water for days,
no matter the cold desert night or with the sun ablaze.

It was just a donkey,
not a newborn lamb of total purity
that a priest could sacrifice with complete sincerity.

It was just a donkey,
a poor man's friend in a rugged, rocky land
of clay-baked soil, oozing mud, or hot burning sand.

Yes, it was just a donkey,
but God made it strong, steadfast, and sturdy,
to carry heavy burdens down dusty roads and not fear getting dirty.

It was just a donkey,
but a trusted, small, and surefooted one
carried Mary to Bethlehem for the birth of God's son.

It was just a donkey,
but it made the long trip to Egypt fleeing Herod's men,
and when Herod died, it brought Jesus' family home again.

It was just a donkey,
but it was chosen by Jesus for his triumphal ride
into Jerusalem when the people waved palms and loud
"Hosannas" cried.

It was just a donkey,
but it was standing in that noisy, motley crowd
when from the cross, "It is finished," its master cried aloud.

It was just a donkey,
a humble, loyal beast, drawn near the cross and there,
drops of Jesus' precious blood fell on its scruffy hair.

It was just a donkey,
but even now a cross of stiff dark hair on each donkey's back
remains,
for the blood from our dear Savior left permanent stains.

Yes, it was just a donkey,
but how like our Lord to choose the lowest of low
to teach us the way we are to be and the way we are to go.

Notes

Mark 15:1–47

Questions

A traveler was weary and needed a place to rest.
He'd been traveling for days and, looking over the hill crest,
he saw a sight that was hard to see.
Criminals were being crucified—he counted three.

People were jeering and milling all around.
One man yelled out, "King of the Jews, why don't you come down?"
He had spoken to the one criminal that had been crowned
with thorns and blood that ran down from his head.
The criminal answered but few heard what he said.

The traveler was drawn to this man; he wasn't sure why.
He didn't usually want to see men die.
His nose rebelled from the smell of hot blood and sweat,
but he couldn't turn away, at least not yet.
He really wanted to hear what the man had to say,
so carefully through the noisy crowd he began making his way.

When suddenly the sky went dark and the earth shook,
the mob instantly grew quiet and started to look
at the man on the center cross and then at each other.
"Over there," one said, "There stands his mother and brother."
Another spoke up, "That group of his followers are praying, but for what?
That imposter is already dead, is he not?"

The traveler looked in the direction of the mother and son.
Their small group was weeping and praying as one.
The traveler made his way toward this very small band.
One man was helping the poor mother to stand.
"Who is this man who was crucified today?" the traveler asked.
But the group all turned away and kept their eyes downcast.

It was a Roman soldier who spoke up and said,
"That far one is a murderer with a price on his head.
The near one is a thief and a scoundrel, I'm told,
and the imposter there in the center is ever so bold.
That lunatic proclaimed he was 'The King of the Jews.'
He was given a chance to recant, but did refuse."
"I heard he's a carpenter and comes from Galilee.
Jerusalem was sure the wrong place for him to be."
These words were spoken by one of the rabble nearby.
"What crime had he committed that meant that he must die?"

The traveler hoped his question wasn't falling on deaf ears.
An old man answered, "It has to do with jealousy and fears.
On the Passover holiday the city is overrun with thieves and insurrectionists.
Besides devote Jews, there are zealots, harlots, and magicians in our midst.
I once heard that man named Jesus enter the synagogue to speak.
He spoke with authority, but was also mild and meek,
but to the priests and elders he's guilty of blasphemy.
He undermines their authority; he is their enemy.
The Romans hope to keep these throngs of people satisfied.
Pilate heard the evidence against Jesus and believed the witnessed lied,
but to keep the peace he freed Barabbas and had Jesus crucified."

The traveler was suddenly overcome with sadness and despair.
He really couldn't understand how he'd come to care
for the man on the center cross whose body now hung still.
Looking up at the cross, the traveler's eyes began to fill
with tears, and his heart seemed to ache in his chest.
His suffering is over, the traveler thought; now he can rest.

The traveler wanted to stay and keep watch at this place,
but he knew it was late and he really must make haste
to find a place to stay before the Sabbath began.
He regretted he hadn't gotten to know the dead man.

He returned to the road and continued on his way,
but he felt compelled to look back and saw the cross sway.
The soldiers were roughly taking the cross down
and apparently planning to put the man on the cold ground.
He started to turn back, but he knew it was no use.
Alone he couldn't stop the soldiers or the crowd from more abuse.
Instead he turned and almost ran from the scene.
He wanted to escape all his eyes had seen.

He wondered if that man would be remembered after today.
Would his followers and friends remember him this way?
Or would they remember him alive and well?
Would they remember his words and others tell?
Would they follow in his footsteps no matter where they would lead?
Would they be willing to be ridiculed, mocked, and to bleed?
Would they overcome their fear and shame and claim him as a friend?
Would they be brave, stand tall, and learn not to bend, or to hide,
or to deny that they followed him?
Would they ever be ready to answer the question that the traveler
asked them—
"Who is that man? Do you know him?"

The following day the traveler was again on his way.
He didn't know that he really needed to stay,
for he missed hearing the very good news
of the miracle, the resurrection of the King of the Jews.

He missed seeing Jesus walking and talking to men.
He missed being with Jesus and seeing his ascension.
He missed Pentecost and missed seeing the Church begin.
He just continued his aimless travel and then,
when finally God's time for him was right,
he met a man named Paul around a campfire one night.

Paul was relating a story of a resurrected Lord.
The traveler was entranced and his questions were his reward.
As he listened he realized he was being told
the story that so vividly in his mind he did hold.
Suddenly tears were streaming down his face,
and he cried, "I was at the cross; I was at that place!"

He was one of those Paul baptized that night,
and they all continued talking and praying until first light.
Now, this traveler didn't stop traveling and his questions remained,
but those questions had become very changed.
Instead of asking, "Who is that man? Do you know him?"
now he asked, "Are you a follower of Jesus? Well, would
you like to know him?"

Notes

Matthew 28:16–20
Mark 15:25–37
Luke 24:1–50
John 20:1–9

When the Time was Right

The cup He had drunk from was still on the table.
Everyone looked at it, but no one was able
to pick it up and put it away,
for each remembered His hand had lifted it only yesterday.

Their own possessions each one carefully took
and left the Upper Room without a second look.
Expecting to be arrested if any were identified,
they slipped quietly from the building to find a safe place to hide.

And so the Sabbath was spent in privacy and seclusion,
a day not of rest, but of total confusion.
The life they had lived had come to an end;
even that fact was hard to comprehend.

They had been together for about three years.
Today all of the shared joys became shared tears.
His death had brought paralyzing grief,
their world was shattered; they questioned their belief.

But they weren't ready to leave each other.
Everyone in their group had become a brother.
And so, in the predawn hours of the first day of the week,
they secretly met with the intention to keep
all of his followers safe from further persecution
by the authorities that controlled by execution.

When all had assembled before the first light,
it seemed apparent several prominent women had taken flight.
For many were leaving and this had to be respected.
The crucifixion of Jesus was totally unexpected.

Their triumphal entrance to the city of Jerusalem
had meant their God was about to deliver them
from their oppression and Jesus would be their earthly king.
He was their Messiah—His coming was no longer a dream.

But now these followers were heartbroken and lost.
Their Jesus had died on a rough-hewn cross.
The suicide of Judas was the first news they shared.
His death seemed so easy when it was compared
to the beatings and cruel treatment Jesus had received.
For the traitor Judas, no one grieved.

Suddenly through the door Mary Magdalene rushed in.
Her searching eyes found Peter and John and then
she spoke to them. But her breathing from running was so erratic,
she appeared to be in a complete panic.

She said several women had taken spices and perfume
to anoint Jesus' body there in his tomb.
But when they'd arrived the large rock was pushed aside,
and Jesus's body was not found on the inside.

Both of these disciples left the safety of their hiding place,
and ran to the Lord's tomb in great haste.
They were dismayed—the tomb was empty, 'twas true.
They knew it now—but they didn't know what they knew.
Peter reported back to those waiting for news.
The women had spoken truth; they weren't confused.

The tomb was empty; Jesus' body had been taken.
Now all of the disciples and followers were further shaken.
Wasn't it enough to see their Lord die?
Why did they steal his body? Why? Why?

These questions were on everyone's mind.
'Twas in the next forty days the answers they'd find.
now they debated on what to do
some most amazing events were about to ensue.

Two followers who'd departed that very morn,
on their way home to Emmaus—both depressed and forlorn—
returned with a story that was difficult to believe.
They told the group there was no reason to grieve,
for Jesus was alive and had been with them.
They'd walked and talked and eaten with Him.

They began to explain how it had all come about
but many in the group were still filled with doubt,
when suddenly Jesus stood among the host.
He startled many who feared He was a ghost.

But His reassuring voice was so wonderful to hear.
He said he was flesh and blood—they had nothing to fear.
He asked for food and ate fish as he had done
so many times before when they'd eaten as one.
Then He opened their minds and they could finally see
what he'd been teaching and what their commission would be.

And then He was gone from that locked room.
Their joy and amazement was more than they could consume.
And so He visited them many times more.
He'd suddenly be in their midst as before,
teaching them and preparing them for what lay ahead,
explaining his death and his rise from the dead,
reminding them to go forth and teach people in every nation,
for Jesus loved them and died for their salvation.

Finally, when the time was right for Jesus to leave,
He took the eleven to the mountain where they'd receive
His final blessing. And then as He ascended into a cloud,
we all need to remember the final words He said aloud,
and they are the most reassuring words I've written on this page:
"And surely I am with you always to the end of the age."

A Searcher's Challenge

Isaiah 45:22
Matthew 6:19–21

The Street Finally Taken Home

I met Sin on the street today.
He was handsome and knew just what to say.
He took my arm and steered me past
the poor, the homeless, and the downcast.

His soothing voice was very sweet.
He told me he would make my life complete.
He said I deserved to concentrate on me.
He said this world could belong to me.

I listened and followed him down the street
where more of his followers I began to meet.
They smiled; they spoke to me when we met.
But each was out to get what he could get.

They cursed, they gossiped, and they lied.
None of them cared if I lived or died.
I began to see that things are truly not enough.
A life is empty when it's only filled with stuff.

I prayed, asked for God's love, and openly confessed.
I turned back to God, and it was the very best
U-turn I've ever made in all my life.
My heart was whole again, my life free of strife.

The street was not so crowded now,
but all I met were quick to ask how
they could help me make my way—
to stay on this road and never stray.

I became happier with every step I took.
Soon I was running and trying to look
for my family and friends who were traveling this way.
More and more of them appeared throughout the day,
and finally I heard my Heavenly Father say,
"Welcome Home, My child, to stay."

Matthew 6:33
Deuteronomy 8:17–18

No Man Can Stop the Wind

Man rushes from place to place—
not a moment can go to waste.
There are endless numbers to be counted;
every wild horse must be mounted.
Tricks and schemes must be quickly detected.
Office holders must duly be elected.

Answers to every question must be found.
There can be no unexpected sight or sound.
Man loves it when a cash register rings.
His mind is constantly on earthly things.
He expects others to see his every endeavor
for it proves to the world he is so clever.

But how foolish this man has become—
thinking he can keep the world under his thumb.
No man can stop the wind,
or change the way the planets spin,
or tell a volcano when to spew,
or order Saturn to add a ring or two.

No man can live beyond his time,
nor can he stop the temperature climb.
He can't count the grains of sand
that are under the ocean or on the land.
He can't eradicate every disease.
He can't even prevent hiccups or stop a sneeze.

If men would only put God first in their lives
and finally begin to carefully prioritize,
God's word would help them truly know,
it's better to be God's disciple than any CEO.

Revelation 3:15–18

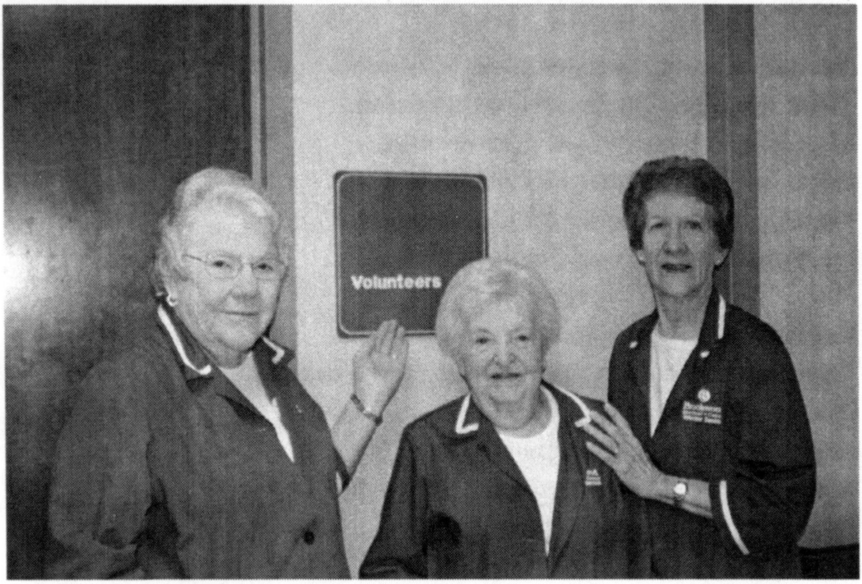

Spectator Christian

Q—Are you a Christian and church member?
A—Yes, for as long as I can remember.

Q—Each Sunday do you sit in a church pew?
A—I've changed churches several times—so more than a few.

Q—Have you attended Sunday School class?
A—Yes, and our class parties are a blast!

Q—Have you given to the poor?
A—I don't know how often—but I've given, I'm sure.

Q—Have you visited the sick or shut in?
A—Yes, and even taken food every now and then.

Q—Have you found time to volunteer?
A—Yes, I gave a number of hours one year.

Q—Do you start each day with prayer?
A—Well, I'm trying, I just haven't quite gotten there.

Q—Do you study your Bible each day?
A—I try, but things sometimes get in my way.

Q—Does your faith continue to grow?
A—I really, really truly hope so.

Q—Have you led anyone to Christ?
A—Well, I brought my neighbor to church once or twice.

Q—Then do you know the God you serve?
A—Of course I do—you've got your nerve.

Q—Have you discovered your spiritual gift?
A—Well, not everyone has talent to inspire and uplift!

Q—Is your name written in God's book?
A—I guess it's there, but I'd be afraid to look!

Notes

Psalms 31:1–5

It's Not Too late

When will I grow up?
When will my temper not erupt?
When will I think before I speak?
When will I learn that I am weak?
When will I control my pride?
When will I put envy aside?
When will I quit making excuses?
When will I use all my creative juices?
When will I put others first?
When will I stay in my God immersed?

Probably not in this lifetime
'cause I'm over seventy and past my prime.
But, Lord I keep trying to please you
in everything I say and do.
Please keep refining me every day,
so that finally there will be a way
that I'm ready to enter Heaven's gate,
and hear St. Peter clearly state,
"Oh, here's a slow learner who had to wait,
but she finally made it and it's not too late."

Proverbs 6:16–19

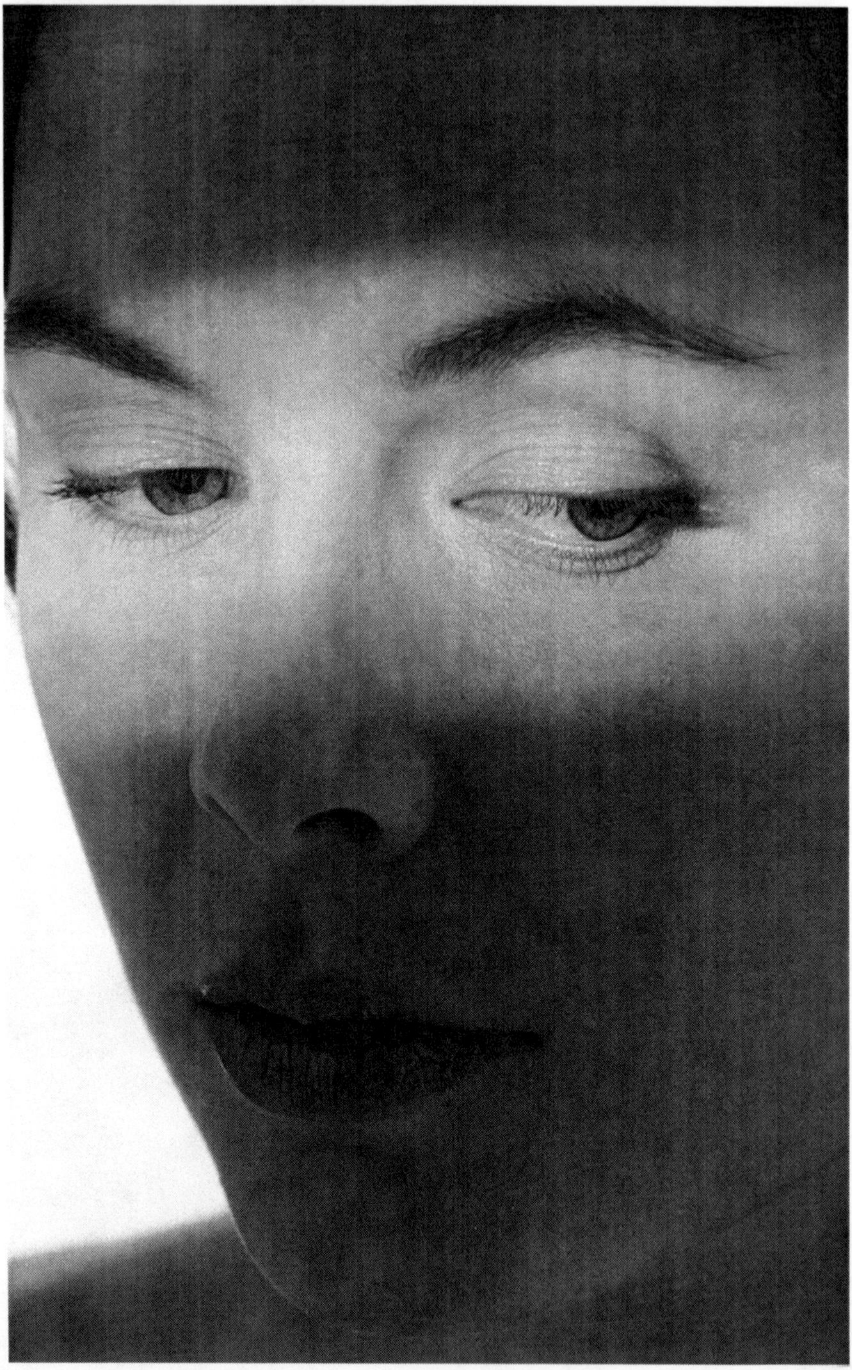

Haughty Eyes

God despises my haughty eyes.
He shakes his head at my white lies.

He hears my every snide remark.
He takes every sin of mine to heart.

He hates it when I fail to pray,
and insist on doing things my way.

He waits patiently for me to confess,
but I'm too busy making another mess.

And then I finally stop and realize—
it all began with my haughty eyes.

Galatians 6:10

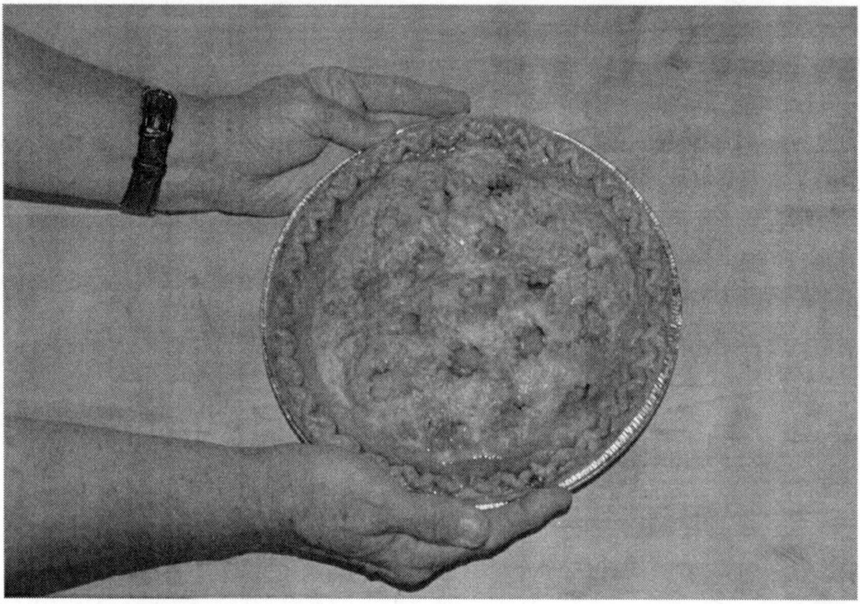

What Can I Bring

The words of a friend might be, "What can I bring?"
The reply is often, "Oh, my, just anything
you like. We all love your strawberry pie
with fresh strawberries piled high,
or the chocolate mousse with the rich Cool Whip,
or even your very hot jalapeño Mexican dip."

How very nice to have the sterling reputation
as a cook whose masterpieces are awaited with great expectation.
But the question, "What can I bring,"
applies to so many, many a thing
besides food and its careful preparation.

What can I bring to a dying friend?
What can I bring to calm a tornado-like wind?
What can I bring to a world thrashing in sin?
What can I bring to a government decaying from within?
What can I bring to the cynical masses?
What can I bring to mend those evil trespasses?
What can I bring to relieve regret?
What can I bring to a mountain of debt?
What can I bring that cannot be lost?
What can I bring that cannot be thrown away or even tossed?

I can bring God's words of his love and the gift of his precious Son
who died for the sins of each and every one.
I can bring His promise of eternal life for all
who confess their sins and for his forgiveness call.
I can be a disciple and a cook who is welcome in every group
because I bring God's good news along with the chicken soup.

Worship and Adoration

Ezekiel 1:26–28
Isaiah 6:1–11

Our Holy Father

Our God sits on a brilliant sapphire throne.
His awesome power and total purity alone
are beyond measure by lowly mortal men,
but are acknowledged by the heavenly seraphim,
who hide their eyes behind one pair of wings
as God's praises each heavenly being sings.
For they know God's fiery eyes are too bright for them,
yet these angels continually rejoice to serve Him.

He is our Holy Father, our Creator, our Lord.
He is to be hallowed, worshipped, and adored
as He sits high in the heavens above
and directs His creation with His all-encompassing love.

I know I am not worthy to speak His name,
but I call on Him daily, just the same.
I know I am not worthy to sing His praise,
yet my hands and voice to Him I freely raise.
I know I'm not worthy to fall on my face to pray,
but I go to Him in prayer each day.
Thank you, dear Holy Father, for allowing me
to praise you, to pray to you, and your child to be.

Deuteronomy 30:20
Psalms 29:3–9

God's Voice

I watch and listen for God's voice,
and when I hear it, I rejoice.

I hear it in a baby's gurgling laugh,
or watching a newborn nursing calf.

Or hearing an eagle's wings soar above,
or listening to a softly cooing dove.

I'm hearing God when the thunder roars,
or crystal clear water over Niagara pours.

Or hearing a church choirs' voices blend,
or hearing a praying child's voice say, "Amen."

And when I hear a psalm or Bible verse,
or hear the lullaby of a baby's nurse,

I know God is expecting me to hear
in my heart as well as in my ear.

God's voice can be heard everywhere.
Its sweetness is beyond compare.

God's telling me that he is here.
He's in control; I need not fear.

Isaiah 48:17–19

God's Way

The road ahead is pitch black.
There is only one thing that I don't lack,
and that's advice from all about me;
my friends all tell me what they see.
Some tell me to take the right.
Obviously this will take me to the light.
Others are sure left is the only way
to get me from this night to day.

But I trust only in my Lord above
who covers me with his perfect love.
I trust he will direct my feet
if only I will solidly keep
my faith, and pray in this dark night
that he will send the brightest light.

For now, I patiently must wait
and not worry that it is getting late.
My time is not God's time, I know,
and to me this wait seems very slow.
But Jesus' words I truly believe—
"Ask and you will receive."
So I continue to read my Bible and pray,
"Great God, let Your Word show me the way."

Acts 20:28

Christ Church

No massive marble columns or even marble floors—
no brass engraved two-storied entrance doors—
no stained glass windows, no silver and no gold—
no palatine steeple where church bells loudly toll—
no lofty organ pipes ringing out melodious sounds—
but our church is a place where God's love abounds.

The church welcomes, soothes, and uplifts each and every one.
It's where we praise God and celebrate His son.
No matter what challenges and disappointments we face
God's loving family here reminds us of God's grace.

It is its people who make Christ Church so strong.
If the devil believes he'll gain a foothold here, he's so very wrong.
For adversity makes us determined to make our lights so shine
that, like Jesus, we'll tell that ol' devil to get behind.

For God's kingdom we will always stand tall.
For God's blood has washed over us all.
Our faith in our Father is completely unshakable.
Our love for each other is clearly unmistakable.
Our people are our marble and our gold.
Our music ministers to the young and the old.

The beauty of our natural surroundings reminds us God is in control.
He sees each heart and he knows each soul.
He will lead us and strengthen us to be a church afire.
He wants us to become a church that will truly inspire.
We know our God has a plan for our church today,
and He will reveal it when we get on our knees and pray.

Ephesians 1:18–19

Heart Eyes

God gave me heart eyes.
They are the perfect size
to see the wrong in my heart to right,
and to see the dark corners I need to light.

I see my failures and successes,
and know my Holy Father blesses
both; for both are ways for me to see
God's love at work in me.

God, keep my heart eyes twenty-twenty
for I'm a master of finding plenty
of hiding places to store my sins,
and my heart I must daily cleanse!

Philippians 2:9–11

Jesus

Jesus is my bedrock.
Jesus is my boat dock.

Jesus is my sunshine.
Jesus is my goldmine.

Jesus is my sailboat.
Jesus is my raincoat.

Jesus is my curtain call.
Jesus is my Christmas ball.

Jesus is my treasure chest.
Jesus is my peaceful rest.

Jesus is my first prize.
Jesus is my sunrise.

Jesus is my best friend.
Jesus is my God send.

Jesus is my savior.

Psalms 105

Call on the Lord

Call on the Lord
when sadness and grief surround you.

Call on the Lord
when there's a fog you can't see through.

Call on the Lord
when your precious children rebel.

Call on the Lord
when there's gossip you wish to tell.

Call on the Lord
when you fear your heart has turned cold.

Call on the Lord
when you need to soothe your soul.

But most of all:

Call on the Lord
when your world is all right.

Call on the Lord
when you are living in the Light.

Call on the Lord
when you don't need to ask for anything.

Call on the Lord
when you can just His praises sing.

Call on the Lord!

Call on the Lord!

Psalms 86

A Renewal

Dear Lord,

Find me;
I'm lost here in the dark.

Guide me through the shadows and thorns
and past the devil's pointed horns.

Surround me here in this dark place
with your awesome love and eternal grace.

Hold my hand and squeeze it tight
and lead me though to your eternal light.

Blind my eyes to the world's glitter and gold,
a false light that can lead me from the fold.

Teach me the words to sing and pray
that will keep me from losing my way.

All this I pray in your precious Son Jesus' name,

Amen

2 Chronicles 7:14

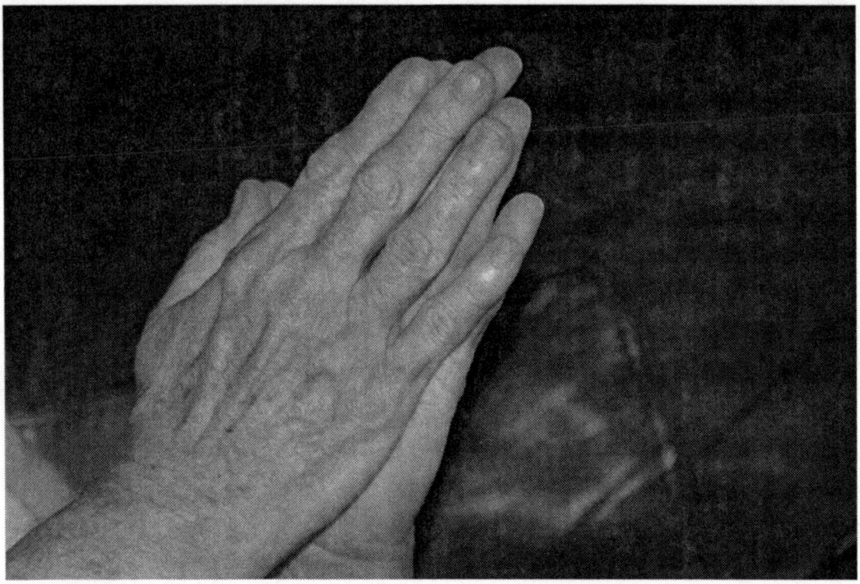

Bedtime Prayer

Dear Lord,

As I lie here and close my eyes to sleep,
I pray that You will comfort me,
and pile my troubles in a heap
and lock them up and lose the key.

I'm much too apt, You know, Lord, to fret and fume
and let the monsters of the night
come fill my heart with fear and gloom
and try to snuff out my trust in Your light.

Lord, I need rest and to have sweet dreams
of times now gone and future days
of happy times, and all good things,
and count my blessings different ways.

But before I sleep, speak loudly, Lord, for I'm too often deaf,
caught in a noisy world going at a frantic pace.
Here in the darkness with none of the day left,
remind me of your love and grace.

Direct my thoughts to ways I can serve.
Put my mind on other's needs.
Make me look forward with pep and verve
to tomorrow's opportunities to do good deeds.

These things I ask in Jesus' name, Amen.

John 14:1–4

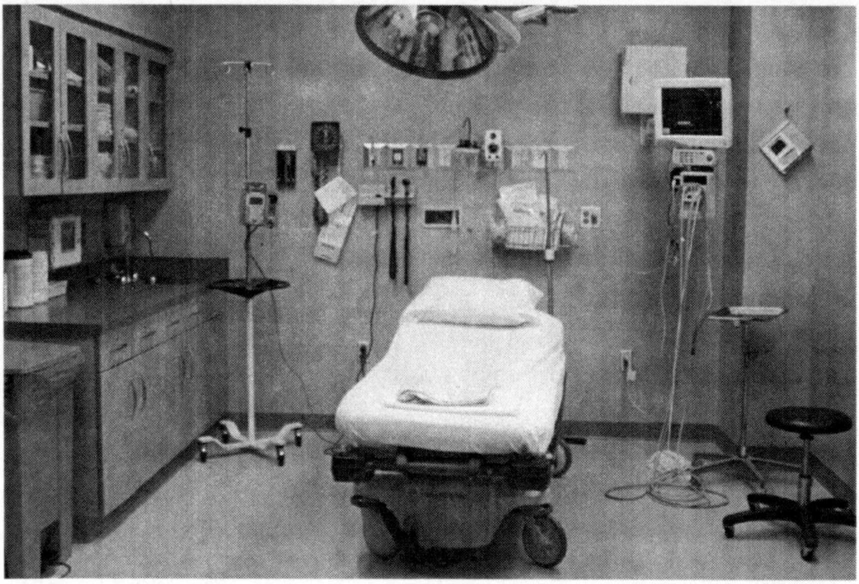

Last Moments

In my last conscious days
just before my earthly eyes glaze
over and my mind becomes confused,
I hope my heart's going to rejoice and refuse
to let any earthly concerns creep in,
for I'll have no more time to pray for them.

My dying moments should be a time of release
from the world's problems that never cease
to a time of calm and trust in my God's promise
of no pain, of no tears, and of complete happiness.
I want to have a smile on my old face
because I know I have been given God's grace.

I hope my soul can hear the angels' song
for then I'll know it won't be long
until I can join the Halleluiah Chorus where
heavenly voices are beyond compare.
In my last moments, let me remember it's a time of celebration,
for dying means I've arrived at my final destination.

Closing Prayer

Jeremiah 29:11–13

Benediction

Dear God,

I pray that this little book
will bring a blessing to all who took
the time to read a poem or two
that you inspired me to write for You.

Let this book find its way
to the nightstand of many, and stay
there to be opened and read now and then
and shared out loud anytime when
it will soothe a suffering soul
whose faith is waning and might grow cold.

These words are words I hope will take
hold in any heart and a stronger Christian make.
These things I ask in your blessed name.

Amen

Author Biography

J. F. Brindley is a retired high school and college English teacher, high school administrator, and mother of three girls. She has written poetry and prose for conferences, workshops, and social events. Finally, after traveling the world with her Air Force officer husband, she has time to begin publishing her work.

Notes

Notes

LaVergne, TN USA
11 March 2011
219793LV00002B/1/P

9 781450 280945